DATE DUE

DEMCO

HIP-HOP

Alicia Keys	Lil Wayne
Ashanti	LL Cool J
Beyoncé	Lloyd Banks
Black Eyed Peas	Ludacris
Busta Rhymes	Mariah Carey
Chris Brown	Mary J. Blige
Christina Aguilera	Missy Elliot
Ciara	Nas
Cypress Hill	Nelly
Daddy Yankee	Notorious B.I.G.
DMX	OutKast
Don Omar	Pharrell Williams
Dr. Dre	Pitbull
Eminem	Queen Latifah
Fat Joe	Reverend Run (of Run DMC)
50 Cent	Sean "Diddy" Combs
The Game	Snoop Dogg
Hip-Hop: A Short History	T.I.
Hip-Hop Around the World	Tupac
Ice Cube	Usher
Ivy Queen	Will Smith
Jay-Z	Wu-Tang Clan
Jennifer Lopez	Xzibit
Juelz Santana	Young Jeezy
Kanye West	Yung Joc

In a career that has lasted more than fifteen years, Nas has earned a reputation for his groundbreaking work. To him, hip-hop is more than about making money.

Nas

Janice Rockworth

Mason Crest Publishers

Nas

Produced by Harding House Publishing Service, Inc.
201 Harding Avenue, Vestal, NY 13850.

MASON CREST PUBLISHERS INC.
370 Reed Road
Broomall, Pennsylvania 19008
(866)MCP-BOOK (toll free)
www.masoncrest.com

Printed in the United States of America

First Printing

9 8 7 6 5 4 3 2 1

Library of Congress Cataloging-in-Publication Data

Rockworth, Janice.
 Nas / Janice Rockworth.
    p. cm. — (Hip-hop)
 Includes bibliographical references and index.
 ISBN 978-1-4222-0300-2
 ISBN: 978-1-4222-0077-3 (series)
 1. Nas (Musician)—Juvenile literature. 2. Rap musicians—United States—Juve-
nile literature. I. Title.
ML3930.N37R63 2008
782.421649092—dc22
[B]
                              2007032969

Publisher's notes:
• All quotations in this book come from original sources and contain the spell-
  ing and grammatical inconsistencies of the original text.
• The Web sites mentioned in this book were active at the time of publication. The publisher is not responsible for Web sites that have changed their
  addresses or discontinued operation since the date of publication. The
  publisher will review and update the Web site addresses each time the book
  is reprinted.

DISCLAIMER: The following story has been thoroughly researched, and to the
best of our knowledge, represents a true story. While every possible effort
has been made to ensure accuracy, the publisher will not assume liability for
damages caused by inaccuracies in the data, and makes no warranty on the
accuracy of the information contained herein. This story has not been autho-
rized nor endorsed by Nas.

Contents

Hip-Hop Time Line   6

1 An Angry Rapper   9

2 Where the Anger
Comes From   19

3 A Boy From the Projects   29

4 The Illest Rapper Around   37

5 A Higher Purpose   47

Chronology   54

Accomplishments and Awards   56

Further Reading/Internet Resources   58

Glossary   60

Index   62

About the Author   64

Picture Credits   64

Hip-Hop Time Line

1970s DJ Kool Herc pioneers the use of breaks, isolations, and repeats using two turntables.

1976 Grandmaster Flash and the Furious Five emerge as one of the first battlers and freestylers.

1984 The track "Roxanne Roxanne" sparks the first diss war.

1988 Hip-hop record sales reach 100 million annually.

1982 Afrika Bambaataa tours Europe in another hip-hop first.

1970s Grafitti artist Vic begins tagging on New York subways.

1980 Rapper Kurtis Blow sells a million records and makes the first nationwide TV appearance for a hip-hop artist.

1985 The film *Krush Groove*, about the rise of Def Jam Records, is released.

1970   1980

1970s The central elements of the hip-hop culture begin to emerge in the Bronx, New York City.

1983 Ice-T releases his first singles, marking the earliest examples of gangsta rap.

1986 Run DMC cover Aerosmith's "Walk this Way" and appear on the cover of *Rolling Stone*.

1979 "Rapper's Delight," by The Sugarhill Gang, goes gold.

1974 Afrika Bambaataa organizes the Universal Zulu Nation.

1984 *Graffitti Rock*, the first hip-hop television program, premieres.

1988 MTV premieres *Yo! MTV Raps*.

1981 Grandmaster Flash and the Furious Five release *Adventures on the Wheels of Steel*.

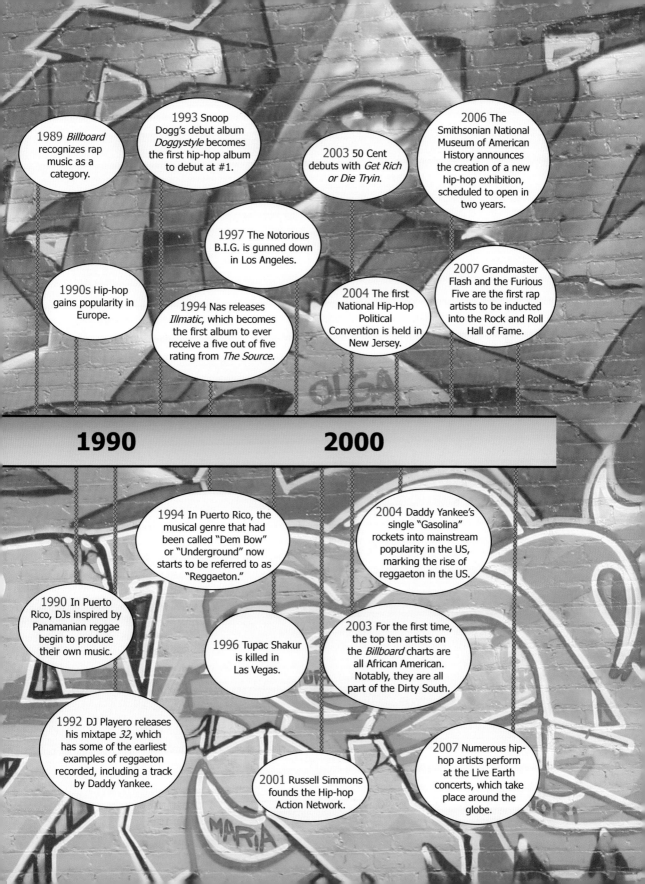

1989 *Billboard* recognizes rap music as a category.

1993 Snoop Dogg's debut album *Doggystyle* becomes the first hip-hop album to debut at #1.

2003 50 Cent debuts with *Get Rich or Die Tryin.*

2006 The Smithsonian National Museum of American History announces the creation of a new hip-hop exhibition, scheduled to open in two years.

1997 The Notorious B.I.G. is gunned down in Los Angeles.

2007 Grandmaster Flash and the Furious Five are the first rap artists to be inducted into the Rock and Roll Hall of Fame.

1990s Hip-hop gains popularity in Europe.

1994 Nas releases *Illmatic,* which becomes the first album to ever receive a five out of five rating from *The Source.*

2004 The first National Hip-Hop Political Convention is held in New Jersey.

1990   2000

1994 In Puerto Rico, the musical genre that had been called "Dem Bow" or "Underground" now starts to be referred to as "Reggaeton."

2004 Daddy Yankee's single "Gasolina" rockets into mainstream popularity in the US, marking the rise of reggaeton in the US.

1990 In Puerto Rico, DJs inspired by Panamanian reggae begin to produce their own music.

1996 Tupac Shakur is killed in Las Vegas.

2003 For the first time, the top ten artists on the *Billboard* charts are all African American. Notably, they are all part of the Dirty South.

1992 DJ Playero releases his mixtape *32,* which has some of the earliest examples of reggaeton recorded, including a track by Daddy Yankee.

2001 Russell Simmons founds the Hip-hop Action Network.

2007 Numerous hip-hop artists perform at the Live Earth concerts, which take place around the globe.

Nas is unique. Some call him "a thinking person's" rapper, spitting out lyrics dealing with deep issues. Many call him a walking contradiction, a description he wouldn't argue with, because he also raps about guns, drugs, and money. But everyone in the hip-hop world calls him talented.

An Angry Rapper

Some rappers seem to only care about guns, drugs, money, and sex. Not Nas. He's a lot deeper. He's a master of words and a poet of the people. Fifteen years ago, his debut album, *Illmatic*, met rave reviews. With that album, Nas showed exceptional lyrical ability. He didn't just spit simple rhymes. His rhymes were complex, thoughtful, and delivered with a unique flow. *Illmatic* is considered one of the most important hip-hop albums ever made. Nas was only nineteen when he made that legendary first album. Since then, he's matured as an individual and an artist. Today, he's still making groundbreaking music and challenging everyone in the hip-hop world to step up their game.

The Art of Contradiction

Nas is now widely recognized as one of hip-hop's most important artists. But his career hasn't always been smooth sailing. He's had ups and downs, with #1 albums followed by highly criticized releases. He's written deep, meaningful songs only to follow with unoriginal, party-hearty affairs. One of the most defining things about Nas is that he's contradictory. In one song, he mourns the violence and hopelessness of ghetto

Like most people in the music industry, Nas's career has had ups and downs. Fortunately, there have been more highs than lows, and he has become one of the most important artists in hip-hop.

life. In another song, he raps about carrying guns and selling drugs. One moment he complains that hip-hop has become a mindless, moneymaking machine. The next moment, he declares everyone might as well jump on the bandwagon and chase the "paper" (rap lingo for cash). Then he reverts to his claim that rappers must remember the history of hip-hop and recommit to the message.

Nas's contradictions can make him difficult to understand. His critics call him "contradictory" as an insult. In an interview for *XXL* magazine, however, Nas explained that he doesn't see being contradictory as a bad thing at all. In fact, he says he welcomes that label, because he sees contradictions as part of being human, living a real life, and creating real art:

> *"I'm totally contradictory. I was gonna make a song called 'Mr. Contradiction.' Cause in essence, it means I'm human. There's not one person in the world that's not a living, walking contradiction. . . . James Brown could say, 'Say it loud, I'm Black and proud,' and then talk about hot pants on another song. Or you know, Marvin [Gaye] could say, 'Let's get it on,' talk about freakish pleasures, whatever you want, but also talk about the world. That makes you whole. . . . Say what you want—I love being a contradiction."*

At the end of the day, Nas's contradictions keep people's attention. They are a major reason why his music has remained complex and thought provoking over the years. Nas will go down in history as one of the most talented and important rappers of his time, and his contradictions will be part of the reason why. Nas's contradictions make him even more interesting as an artist because they reflect hip-hop music as a whole.

A Reflection of the Music

Hip-hop music can be intelligent, poetic, influential, and inspiring. It can also be violent, obscene, and *discriminatory*. Some hip-hop songs call for people to unite in a spirit of love and brotherhood. Others are filled with sexist lyrics, gay bashing, and racist commentary. Sometimes hip-hop music speaks seriously and mournfully about the effects of guns, drugs, and "live fast, die young" attitudes. Other times the songs are all about partying, often with guns, drugs, and recklessness in tow.

Even with all its contradictions, however, hip-hop music is some of the most popular music in the world. It has become a defining part of North American culture. It is also popular all over the world. Rap music is popular in Asia, Africa, South America, and Europe, with each region boasting its own "homegrown" artists and hip-hop cultures.

Nas has been a player in the hip-hop game for more than fifteen years. In that time, he's had #1 albums and commercial failures. He's had extremely loyal fans, and perhaps equally loyal critics. He suffered a career slump only to come back and reestablish himself as one of the most important voices in the industry. Through it all, he has survived to become one of the longest lived and most respected MCs around. But to understand Nas as a legendary rapper, we need to also understand the music that he makes: hip-hop.

The Tradition of Hip-Hop Music

Hip-hop music has been around since the 1970s, when it started in America's inner cities. The first hip-hop music developed at house and block parties in the Bronx, a borough of New York City. It was created by DJs and MCs. DJs made the music by cutting and mixing beats from popular dance songs (mostly *funk*, disco, and soul songs). MCs rhymed to the music, creating a new lyrical style called rapping. The result—a

DJs were king during hip-hop's earliest days. They spun the tunes, mixing and scratching to get the people up on the dance floor. More important, their skills kept the people dancing. Eventually MCs came to the forefront and technology took over much of the DJ's former responsibility.

beat-heavy music with a uniquely urban sound—spread like wildfire throughout New York City and then to other cities all over North America.

A lot of people who heard hip-hop in those early days wrote it off as a passing fad. After all, how could music in which no one played an instrument and no one sang last? But those early skeptics were very wrong. Hip-hop wasn't a passing fad. In fact, over the next three decades, it would become the voice of generations of young people around the world.

Hip-hop developed during a difficult period in American history, and the music spoke to young people from the inner city. The 1970s were a frustrating time for many Americans. The Vietnam War raged until 1975. An oil embargo sparked an energy crisis that crippled the economy. After the Watergate scandal, President Richard Nixon was forced to resign the presidency, leaving Americans disgusted with politics and their faith in America's leaders at an all-time low. There was a general mood of discontent in the country, and that mood was far worse in the inner city.

The Inner City: Ripe for Revolution

By the 1970s, America's inner cities had been crumbling for decades. As wealthier people and the businesses that served them moved to the suburbs, America's cities went into rapid decline. Poor, largely minority, populations were left behind to face falling property values, aging buildings, declining schools, and reduced services. Many poor people lived in publicly funded housing projects. The projects often had substandard living conditions, were poorly built, and suffered from overcrowding. For some living in projects, life within their home was almost as dangerous as the streets as the crackerjack-box type housing units became the site of increasing crime rates.

By the time hip-hop music developed, many of the people

living in America's cities were frustrated. Young people in the inner cities saw a world filled with poverty, crime, drugs, and hopelessness. Worse yet, they saw that few people cared about the decaying neighborhoods, and even fewer opportunities for a better life existed. For these young people, hip-hop was a bright light in a dark world. It gave them a voice.

Hip-hop music was all about expression, rebellion, challenge, and respect. MCs spit rhymes about their superior rapping skills and their daring exploits on the streets. Freestyle battles, in which MCs made up rhymes on the spot, could spring up just about anytime, anywhere. A good freestyle rapper could gain great respect in his neighborhood. Rapping became a way for young people to talk about their world, rebel against their circumstances, challenge each other, and earn reputations and local fame.

Hip-hop music and **culture** spread around the country. The most popular topics for rappers to rhyme about were their own skills as MCs and the weaknesses of their rivals. Rappers also spit tales of ghetto life, rapping about common themes like poverty, crime, playing the numbers (a popular but illegal form of lottery), and drugs. By the 1980s, the first popular rap songs were hitting the airwaves.

"Black Music"

By the 1980s, hip-hop had a firm reputation as "black music." It was a reputation, however, that wasn't completely accurate. Yes, hip-hop music was especially popular among black people, but from the very beginning, hip-hop musicians and fans came from many backgrounds. Latino artists, for example, have played an important role in hip-hop music from its very birth in the black and Latino neighborhoods of the South Bronx.

Hip-hop music isn't just black music, but there is a good reason for that perception. Hip-hop is the music of all disenfranchised people. Disenfranchised is a very big word, but it has a very simple meaning: powerless. A disenfranchised person is a person whose voice and influence have been taken away (or were never granted in the first place). One of the most extreme examples of disenfranchisement is when people are denied the right to vote. For example, black men were denied the right to vote (or were disenfranchised) until shortly after the Civil War. Women of all races were denied the right to vote until much later, 1920.

Despite the many freedoms people in the United States have, they have not always been given easily or equally. That inequality helped create the climate that led to the birth of hip-hop.

Being denied the right to vote isn't the only form of disenfranchisement people can experience. Any situation or condition that denies people their rights or reduces their ability to have a voice in society and government is a form of disenfranchisement. In America, minority groups have historically suffered from disenfranchisement. And the some of the most disenfranchised people have been black people.

Righteous Anger

The first rap songs on popular radio were lighthearted, party songs. But on the streets, hip-hop music had developed a decidedly political bent. In 1982, Grandmaster Flash and the Furious Five released one of hip-hop music's first political anthems. It was called "The Message," and with lyrics like "Got a bum education, double-digit inflation/Can't take the train to the job, there's a strike at the station," it spoke of real-world struggles.

But hip-hop music didn't just become political in the eighties. It also became angry. In 1988, the South Central Los Angeles group, N.W.A., shocked the nation with their lyrics about killing police officers. Their songs got N.W.A. labeled the "World's Most Dangerous Group." They also showed that many hip-hop artists were filled with rage. Anger is still a defining part of hip-hop music today, and artists like Nas continue to express that anger in their songs.

Many people, especially people who are not hip-hop fans, can't understand why rappers like Nas are so angry. But the people who began hip-hop music had lots to be angry about. They came from some of the worst inner-city neighborhoods in America. They faced the effects of hundreds of years of racism, inequality, and **oppression** all around them. Hip-hop music didn't just appear one day out of the blue. It was borne from a long history of struggle and frustration. To understand why hip-hop music is so angry, you must understand the history of oppression and racism in America.

Some hip-hop artists drew from the anger that they saw growing around them. Artists like Nas wrote lyrics that reflected the frustration felt by many in their neighborhoods.

Where the Anger Comes From

We often call America the "land of the free and home of the brave." Throughout its history, America has been a world leader in democracy and freedom. From laws that forbid child labor to technologies that improve health and life, Americans have a lot to be proud of. But with so many successes to focus on, it can be easy to look at American history through rose-colored glasses. America certainly has triumphs. But like all places, it also has struggles, failures, and incidences of extreme cruelty. If you don't know about these darker aspects of American history, you will never truly understand hip-hop music or an artist like Nas.

A History of Powerlessness and Oppression

Nas and many other hip-hop artists rap about inequality, poverty, racism, and other hardships affecting their communities. Those hardships are not new. They are part of the fabric of American society, and can be traced all the way back to America's beginnings. Rappers' lyrics often express anger, saying their communities (especially black communities) are disenfranchised and their people treated as second-class citizens. That disenfranchisement and second-class treatment began when black people were first brought to America as slaves, and it has continued in many different forms throughout American history.

At the end of the Civil War, slavery was finally abolished throughout the entire United States. It was supposed to be a new dawn for black people in America. In reality, however, many things did not improve, especially in the South. People were freed from slavery, but they still had no land, no money, and no real access to education. For many, the life as a slave on farms and plantations continued, except now they were called sharecroppers instead of slaves. For others, it continued in poorly paid domestic employment as maids, nannies, washerwomen, drivers, and similar jobs. America's black people now had freedom, but they still had little hope for a better life.

Furthermore, racism and brutality were everywhere, and black people's lives were still ruled by fear and intimidation. In the South, "Jim Crow" laws required that white and black people be separated. Those laws made life very difficult for black people and condemned them to second-rate treatment and services (despite the stated emphasis on "separate but equal"). But what was even worse was a spirit of vicious, racist lawlessness in which out-of-control mobs regularly lynched people (particularly black men) for even the most minor misstep. Just speaking to or looking at a white woman could be enough to get a black man lynched. Sometimes just being in the wrong place at the wrong time was enough for a black man to be dragged off, beaten, hanged, and burned.

Looking for a New Life

By the early twentieth century, black people were leaving the South in droves. Black people had begun moving to America's

The Harlem section of New York City went from being the site of an important art, music, and literary movement to become run-down, drug infested, and crime ridden. Today Harlem is on an upswing, but it is now too expensive for many longtime residents to live there.

Northern cities shortly after the Civil War. They hoped to find higher-paying jobs, better education, and more equality in urban areas. In the early part of the twentieth century, the trickle of black people moving to Northern cities became a sudden gush. In fact, so many people flowed into America's cities that the time period (about 1910–1930) was named "The Great Migration."

For the first time, large, mostly black neighborhoods developed in Northern cities. Some people were successful in finding better jobs and moving into the lower-middle and middle classes. In fact, in the twenties and thirties, black America experienced something called the Harlem Renaissance. As some black Americans began advancing in American society, they had new opportunities in art and education. A cultural explosion of black scholarship, literature, music, and art followed.

The Harlem Renaissance continued into the 1930s, but as the Great Depression unfolded and World War II flared, hard times returned. In fact, for most black Americans, the hard times had never left. While some individuals found success in Northern cities, many did not. Black people from the South were, generally speaking, already at a disadvantage in Northern cities. After a lifetime of oppression, lack of education, and poor job opportunities, they had a harder time competing for jobs. Even when black people could find more meaningful employment, they were often paid less than white people.

Slavery may have been outlawed, but racism was still everywhere, and sometimes black people were simply denied the better jobs, no matter how experienced or educated they were. The North may not have had the lynchings of the South, but discrimination still ruled black people's lives, and the cycle of poverty that black people had been trapped in for so long continued. The frustration the black community had now felt for well over a century continued to grow. One day, that frustration would pour into the lyrics of hip-hop music, but that was still a few decades away. In the meantime, more changes would take place and shape America's inner cities into launch pads for hip-hop music.

"White Flight" and America's Changing Cities

For many years, America's cities were robust hubs of economic and social activity. Their bright lights and promise of good jobs drew people in, and the cities grew and prospered. After World War II ended, however, American cities began to change. As something called "white flight" began, America's urban areas went into a slow and steady decline that, in many areas, would continue into the 1990s. In some cities, in fact, the urban decay even continues today.

White flight was the movement of white and wealthier populations out of the cities and into the suburbs. After World War II, huge highway and freeway projects began opening up America, triggering a suburban boom. Racism was still a defining part of American society, and some white people fled the downtowns because of hatred and fear of black people. Others, however, left simply because suburbs seemed like the ideal place to live. The suburbs, with their picket fences, green lawns, and wide, quiet streets seemed more inviting than the concrete, high rises, and noise of the downtown.

Whether people left the city because of their racist beliefs or left simply because the suburbs seemed like a nicer place to live, the effect was the same. White and wealthier populations left metropolitan areas. Black and poor populations remained behind. And businesses go where the money is. So as the white and the wealthy vacated downtowns, businesses followed. They set up shop around the suburbs. Malls and strip malls were born. Soon there was no reason to go into the city at all. Many cities, starved of the people and businesses that paid property taxes and fueled the economy, went into steady decline.

During the 1950s and 1960s, many once-prosperous inner cities became dilapidated, as those who could moved to the suburbs. The inner cities were left to some of the communities' poorest. Before long, people's dreams of the future turned just as bleak as their surroundings.

People in poor, black, urban communities didn't have the same freedom as wealthy, white people to leave the decaying urban areas. Many people didn't have the money for suburban life. The money it took to rent an apartment and pay bus fare wasn't anywhere near enough for a house in the suburbs and a car to get around. Furthermore, many banks in that era had racist lending policies and denied mortgages and loans to black people or people living in certain neighborhoods. So, even black people with a high enough income couldn't get a mortgage or loan. Plus, even those black families who could afford to move to the suburbs often faced **intimidation** and even violence once they got there, as angry white residents tried to drive them out.

Inner Cities in Flames

By the 1950s, racism was still as pervasive as ever around the country. Jim Crow laws were still in effect. Lynchings still occurred. But racism didn't have to be so obvious to be damaging, and many much subtler forms of racism existed. A memory from a woman interviewed for this book shows how racist beliefs found their way into even the simplest parts of everyday life. In the 1950s, as a young girl growing up in a Northern city, she attended an all-white, Catholic elementary school. She remembers learning the following folk song for a school concert:

The Watermelon Song

You can talk about your apples, your peaches, and your pears
Your cinnamon hanging on a cinnamon tree
But bless your heart my honey, it's very plain to see
That watermelon am the fruit for me.

Yes sir oh, hambone am sweet
Chicken am good
Possum meat am very, very fine, ain't it so
But give me, oh give me, I really wish you would
That watermelon hanging on the vine.

And when I went to fetch it, twas on a rainy night
The moon had not as yet begun to shine
And though the white man saw me, and shot me through the fence
I'll never get that melon on the vine.

The song is about a black person stealing a watermelon, and its lyrics are filled with racial **stereotypes**. Among them, that black people speak poor English, love watermelon, are prone to criminal behaviors like stealing, and are at the mercy of primal desires (represented by wanting watermelon so badly, one is willing to get shot for it). The song is actually an example of racist stereotypes, some simply ignorant, others more vicious, wrapped up in an innocent, pleasant-sounding folk song. In the mid-twentieth century, schools generally saw nothing wrong with teaching this song in their classrooms. It's just one small example of how common racism and preju-dicial thinking were in everyday life, and how easily young minds were shaped to continue thinking in racial stereotypes.

By this time in the country's history, black Americans had had enough. The civil rights movement was well under way, attempting to change the discriminatory laws, institutions, and attitudes that shaped black people's lives and continued their oppression. The civil rights movement made great strides, perhaps most notably the abolishment of Jim Crow laws. But the civil rights movement also met great resistance, and when important leaders like Malcolm X and Dr. Martin Luther King Jr. were murdered, black people around the country were en-raged. After Dr. King's death in 1968, riots exploded around the country. As the seventies rolled in, America's inner cities were smoldering in the ashes of generations of racism, poverty, and brutal disenfranchisement. Hip-hop was born out of these angry ashes, and lifetimes of discrimination would find voice in the angry voices of its rappers.

Some people might have become swallowed up by feelings of despair, but others, like Nas, turned his childhood experiences of poverty and the projects into the lyrics of hip-hop hits.

A Boy From the Projects

Queensbridge Houses is a housing project in New York City's borough of Queens. With more than three thousand units, for many years it was the largest public housing project in the United States. It has also been the childhood home of many rappers. The project was built in the late thirties, but by the 1970s, Queensbridge's buildings were dilapidated, worsening the already cramped conditions. With a *diverse* mix of tenants, including large white, black, and Latino populations, racial tensions often flared. It wasn't the best place to grow up, but it gave budding hip-hop artists lots to rap about. One day, it would be fertile ground for Nas's rhymes.

Nas the Boy

On September 14, 1973, Nasir Jones was born in Brooklyn, New York. One day he would write a song, "Fetus," describing his journey to this world. In the song, his parents are conflicted about his coming and consider having the pregnancy aborted. Nas raps, "pops took moms to see the doc at the clinic, but I was saved cause he changed his mind in the last minute/. . . While they broke up furniture and smashed plates on the wall, I wondered if I am born will I be safe at all."

Nasir Jones—Nas—grew up in the New York City borough of Queens. Home for the young boy and his family was Queensbridge Houses, a low-income housing project. Later, as a rap star, Nas put together an album with the project's former residents who had gone on to a career in hip-hop.

By the end of the song, however, the young couple is overjoyed to see their son arrive. Nas was indeed born to proud parents, and he would have close relationships with both of them. His mother, Fannie Ann Jones, worked for the post office. His father was jazz musician Olu Dara. Music was an important part of Nas's life from his earliest days. His father played the trumpet, and he listened intently to his father's music and began playing the trumpet himself when he was still very young.

Nas was still just a small child when his family moved from Brooklyn to the Queensbridge projects. Hip-hop music was exploding in the projects, and Nas would listen to it throughout his childhood. But Nas didn't want to be a rapper at first. For a long time, he wanted to follow in his father's footsteps as a musician. Nas was luckier than a lot of kids he knew in the projects. Yes, his father traveled a lot, often leaving the family for extended periods of time while he toured, but Nas still knew his father and received a lot of guidance from him. In an interview for the article "Bridging the Gap," posted at theavemagazine.com, Nas and Olu spoke openly about the early years of Nas's life. Nas described how important it was to have his father around:

> *"So many of my peers grew up without their fathers. They never had that tight structure in the household with a man there, so a lot of them are wild and crazy. I always thought of that and felt bad for them. I couldn't imagine that being my story. So that alone made the relationship [with my dad] golden."*

And his father influenced him in other ways as well. Olu traveled extensively throughout Europe and Africa, so he had knowledge about the world that he could share with his sons. And although Olu Dara was best known for his musical abilities, he was also an actor and writer. Following in his father's footsteps, Nas began writing short stories and poetry at a young age. He also loved to draw. At one point in his childhood, he decided he wanted to become a comic book artist.

Young Talent

But Nas also fell in love with the hip-hop music he heard exploding all around him. Soon he was writing raps of his own, and he was participating in another aspect of hip-hop culture: dancing. B-boying, or break dancing, was a major part of hip-hop in the eighties. Other forms of street dancing, like popping and locking, were also popular. Nas began dancing under the b-boy name "Kid Wave."

Olu could see that Nas had many talents, and he encouraged his son's interests. In the "Bridging the Gap" article, Olu remembers Nas's childhood interest in hip-hop culture:

> *"I took Nas to Lincoln Center to see one of the first rap movies. It could have been Krush Groove or something like that. And I remember Nas seeing LL Cool J walk by with a radio on his shoulder. Nas was young and he said, 'Daddy, he's gonna be a star.' I didn't know who the hell LL was, but Nas was always particular about predicting who's gonna be a star. Once, he picked up a Michael Jackson album, Off the Wall, he said, 'He's gonna be big, big, big, big daddy!'"*

It seems Nas had an eye for talent and an ear for music even from his earliest years. Not everything, however, was happy in Nas's young life. His father spent lots of time away from the family while he toured. Soon, it was apparent to Nas that his mother and father weren't getting along. When Nas was thirteen years old, his parents separated. He and his younger brother, Jabari, continued to live with their mother, but their father moved out. Watching his parents' marriage crumble was devastating, and Nas would later rap about that sadness in the song "Poppa Was a Player." In it, he talks about his father staying out late and chasing other women, but he also forgives his father in the song and shows respect for the parents who struggled to do the best for their kids, even if they couldn't do the best for each other.

"Kid Wave" and "Ill Will"

When Nas was a teenager, Queensbridge native Marley Marl was shaking up the hip-hop world with his group, the Juice Crew. Hip-hop music, once only heard at parties or on *mixtapes* sold out of people's cars, was moving to the radio. Rappers were actually getting record deals. It was becoming clear, at least to a few people, that hip-hop wasn't just a fad, and some kids were now dreaming of becoming big stars as MCs.

Nas was one of those kids. He was a smart kid with lots of talent, but school wasn't holding his attention. He dropped out in the eighth grade. He continued to read and educate himself (he was especially interested in black history and religion, particularly Islam), but he started pursuing other interests, primarily rap. He no longer dreamed of being a comic book artist or jazz musician. Now he wanted to be a rapper.

At first Nas was afraid to rap in front of other people. He was a quiet kid with deep thoughts, and he wrote a lot of personal lyrics. He didn't know if other people would understand his songs or like what he wrote. But he knew he had to conquer that fear. He made his mind up to be an MC. But he needed a DJ. He knew the perfect person. His best friend, Willie Graham, lived upstairs in their Queensbridge building. Willie became "Ill Will" the DJ, and together, the two began their lives as hip-hop artists.

"Nasty Nas"

The young MC and DJ were just teenagers, but they were already sniffing for their first record deal. That, however, was hard to land. But Nas did land a big break in 1991 when he was invited to drop a line on the song "Live at the Barbeque" by the hip-hop crew Main Source. The song appeared on their first album, *Breaking Atoms*. Nas's voice was on wax, a major milestone. After that, Nas began developing a following, especially on the New York scene, but he still couldn't land that record deal.

Like many kids his age, the young Nas wanted to be a rapper. He became MC Kid Wave, and his friend Willie Graham was Ill Will, the DJ, spinning the albums. Teens Kid Wave and Ill Will then went looking for a record deal.

Then, a year after his first appearance on wax, tragedy struck. Nas's best friend and musical partner, Willie "Ill Will" Graham, fell victim to the tragedy of the ghetto. He was shot and killed in the Queensbridge projects the boys called home. Nas was only eighteen years old, and he now knew firsthand how lives could begin and end in violence and tragedy in the projects.

His best friend's death came just as Nas's career was beginning to turn a corner. Nas, who now went by the MC name "Nasty Nas" (he would shorten it to simply "Nas" later), finally scored that first record deal with Columbia. He appeared on some **tracks** with other artists, and he began work on his own solo album. On April 19, 1994, that album dropped. It was called *Illmatic*, and it would change everything.

With his first album declared a masterpiece, Nas was on his way as a rapper. He made what some critics thought were less than smart career moves. Even some of his first fans weren't sure they liked some of the directions he was taking with his music.

4

The Illest Rapper Around

Illmatic wasn't a huge seller, but the numbers don't represent the album's value. Some people immediately called it a masterpiece, both of music and of lyrics. But it would take time to tell the album's true importance. Years later, it would be clear. *Illmatic* is an album that helped re-energize and redefine hip-hop music, and it will go down in history as one of the most significant hip-hop albums ever recorded.

In the early nineties, when *Illmatic* was released, gangsta rap was taking over the hip-hop scene. To the dismay of many hip-hop fans and critics, gangsta rap seemed to be replacing hip-hop's political and socially conscious messages with glorifications of guns, drugs, and violence. The trend would continue well into the new millennium, but occasionally albums like *Illmatic* surfaced. Those albums reminded listeners that hip-hop music could be about deeper things: the life and death struggles of the streets, the complex interplay of triumph and tragedy in everyday life, the ability of people born into poverty and disadvantage to use their experiences to strengthen themselves, rise above, and conquer all.

Going Mainstream, Getting Backlash

Illmatic put Nas on the hip-hop map, but it didn't get him much recognition on **mainstream** radio. That was soon to come. In July of 1996, Nas released his second solo album, *It Was Written*. The album shocked a lot of his fans. It had a far more **commercial**, pop-friendly sound. The sound attracted scores of new fans, and the album flew off the shelves. But those fans who had loved Nas as a gritty, **underground** artist accused him of selling out. He got criticism for another reason as well. On the album, he adopted a "Mafioso rap" **persona** and called himself "Nas Escobar."

Mafioso rap was quickly becoming some of the most popular rap music of the nineties. It was a spin-off of gangsta rap. But in the Mafioso style, rappers drew comparisons between themselves and mobsters, portraying themselves as larger-than-life characters who used crime to finance a life of luxury. Many critics didn't want to see Nas, whose messages had seemed so deep and meaningful in his previous work, cross over to the Mafioso style. Nevertheless, the album shot to #1 on the *Billboard* 200 album chart and went on to sell more than three million copies. At this time, Nas also joined a group of other hip-hop artists to create a crew called The Firm. They released an album in 1997, but broke up soon after.

Nas also had his first film experience in this period. He had always liked to write, and he joined with Hype Williams to co-write a film called *Belly*. The film, about two drug dealers who go down separate paths, was released in 1998. Nas was the narrator and had a starring role, along with fellow rapper DMX.

After *Belly*, it was back to music for Nas. In 1999, he released *I Am . . .*, his third solo album, which received more criticism from hardcore fans who felt Nas was still selling out to get popular appeal. Nevertheless, the album debuted at #1 on the *Billboard* 200, and it went on to sell more than two million copies. The album was originally supposed to be a two-disc release, but a lot of songs were cut after they were leaked to the Internet as mp3s. Nas later released a lot of that original material on an album called *The Lost Tapes*.

The major Internet leak, however, wasn't the biggest story surrounding the album. The biggest story was over the controversial video for the single "Hate Me Now." The original video showed Nas and featured guest Puff Daddy being crucified. Puff Daddy later objected and was edited out of the video. Later in the year, Nas released another album, *Nastradamus*, but it received poor reviews and much lower sales (although it would eventually go **platinum**).

Getting in the Industry, Getting into Beef

After *Nastradamus*'s lackluster performance, things went quiet on the solo-album front. But Nas was busy in other ways. He was getting in the studio with other artists, trying to jump-start careers for rappers signed to his new company, Ill Will Records (a Columbia Records imprint named for his best friend, Willie Graham). Bravehearts, a rap crew headed up by Nas's younger brother (who goes by the MC name, Jungle), is signed to Ill Will Records. In 2000, the imprint released a **compilation** album called *Nas and Ill Will Records Present QB's Finest*, featuring artists from Queensbridge Houses.

Perhaps the biggest development in Nas's career at this time, however, was a beef he had going with hip-hop **icon**, Jay-Z. In the hip-hop world, "beefing," or feuding with other rappers, seems to just be part of the culture. Usually these beefs are just wars of words (primarily on diss tracks), and they can even be good for rappers, challenging them to outdo each other using wit and rhyme. But while some beefs, like the one between Nas and Jay-Z, allow two powerful rappers to prove their skills as intelligent and talented MCs, others simply dissolve into the trading of ridiculous, immature insults. Even worse, beefs sometimes end in real violence.

The beef between Nas and Jay-Z, however, seemed to spark both men's careers. When Nas came out with the diss track

One of the biggest and most important names in hip-hop history is Jay-Z. Nas and Jay-Z participated in one of hip-hop's most famous beefs, each artist dissing the other. That didn't stop Nas from signing with Jay-Z's label after they ended their beef.

"Ether," fans went wild. The track seemed to bring back a lot of Nas's underground, street **credibility**. It helped renew hardcore fans' faith in their man. In 2001, their faith grew even more when Nas released his fifth studio album, *Stillmatic*. The album brought Nas full circle, returning him to the deeper subject matter and street lyrics of his *Illmatic* days. It didn't go over as well in the mainstream, pop-hip-hop world, but it put Nas back on top as one of the most respected artists in the game.

A God of Hip-Hop

After releasing *Stillmatic*, Nas never again wavered. It seemed that he had finally found his place as an artist. That place was in music that spoke about meaningful things, not in chasing paper with pop-friendly tunes or catering to the masses with Mafioso fantasies.

On his Web site, godsson.net, Nas explained that for him, making music is not about the money:

> *"I make money from what I do, and it's God's gift. I didn't get in the business just to make a million or two billion overnight. There's nothing wrong with that, but I don't care. I just love the music and enjoying my life at the same time. I love rap more than being a star in rap."*

Nas went back into the studio and started recording his sixth studio album. But there was tragedy in his life. His mother was dying of breast cancer, and she passed away before the album was completed. Nas poured his emotions into his songs, and when he released *God's Son*, it was in many ways a tribute to his mother. Many believed it was his most mature album to date, showing an artist walking away from material concerns for a higher, spiritual level. The single "I Can" reminds young black people about their proud history, warns them of the dangers in everything from the streets to media messages, and encourages them to follow their dreams and reach their full potential. In the song, Nas raps, "Nobody says you have to be gangstas . . . /Read more, learn more, change the globe." It became the biggest hit of Nas's career.

God's Son was a defining moment in Nas's career. His Web site, godsson.net, calls the album "a portrait of a young man struggling with his demons, yet open to the possibility of angels." It also quotes Nas explaining the album saying, "My goals are to live well and be at peace until I leave this raggedy [world]. This is a [beautiful] world if you can deal with all the [terrible things], it's a beautiful world." Just one month after its release, *God's Son* went platinum.

Street's Disciple

Nas's career was supercharged again. Reinvigorated, he went back into the studio embarking on a major project with a big message. It would be a two-disc album, and following through with the spirit shown in *God's Son*, it would be filled with political messages. Nas released *Street's Disciple* on November 30, 2004. The album did go platinum (Nas's seventh to do so), but it actually didn't do as well commercially as expected. Nevertheless, Nas feels that it was some of his best work. In an interview with MTV.com, Nas explained that, despite the criticism, he feels the album is really worth its salt:

"That album was a milestone period for me. It was my triumph in this business. The focus for that last record was definitely not about what was going on at radio at the time. It was about me doing different stuff. With the next stuff I'm getting at, it's gonna be right up that alley, but a huge project. I want to get back to doing real big [stuff] for the streets."

Street's Disciple went platinum, but sales dipped. Despite disappointing sales, though, Nas is proud of the album. He considers it some of his best work. Many critics agree.

Street's Disciple cemented Nas's place as one of the most important political and socially conscious voices in hip-hop today. Many critics mourn how empty so much hip-hop music has become. That rage that defined early hip-hop music has been largely lost, sold out to bling and paper chasing. For all those who mourned hip-hop's current state, *Street's Disciple* was reason for hope. The *San Francisco Bay Guardian*, in fact, called the album the "one notable exception by

Nas had grown up around music, especially jazz; his father was a jazz musician. On *Street's Disciple*, Nas celebrates blues and jazz, two music forms that played important roles in the development of hip-hop.

a commercial artist" in a hip-hop world that seems to have lost all its rage and political willpower, and said the album, "sternly takes political and public icons to task."

Street's Disciple also sought to place hip-hop music in historical perspective by connecting it to its roots in other "black music" like blues and jazz. To do this, the album features Nas's father, jazz musician Olu Dara, on the single "Bridging the Gap." In the interview for their "Bridging the Gap" article, Nas stated that the song with his father wasn't just about the music. It was also about presenting their father/son relationship as an example for others. He talked about why he feels it's so important to show the world the close relationship he has with his father:

> *"My father was a great father. That's why we had to make this record as an example for the kids whose fathers were either shot down in the street or taken down by the prison systems or drugs. We have to let them know, alright, those brothers are gone, but it's up to us now to break the chain, break the cycle and become incredible, strong family structures for our future."*

It's another example of how far Nas has come in his career. He no longer sees himself as simply a rapper, and he no longer sees rap music as just a way to support himself and make money. Now he sees himself as a leader of the people, and rap music as his word. Nas understands what many of the great hip-hop artists who came before him knew: that hip-hop rose out of centuries of struggle, and now it has the power to raise people.

As Nas has matured as an individual and an artist, he has adjusted his attitude as well. He's decided not to be the first one to throw down a diss, and he's critical of the way hip-hop seems to all sound the same.

A Higher Purpose

Nas's new attitude, which focuses on knowledge, inspiration, and empowerment, can also be seen in the way he now conducts his career. After their vicious war, he buried the hatchet with Jay-Z, a move that was a great example to other rappers, encouraging them to unite instead of fight. In 2006, Nas even signed with Jay-Z's label, Def Jam.

Can't Escape the Beef

Today, Nas is critical of the beefs so prevalent in hip-hop, although he's not entirely above the conflict. He still gets drawn into the culture of beefing and dissing, but he's clearly a reluctant participant. In his mtv.com interview, Nas explained that he'll give it back if someone takes a swipe at him, but it's certainly not his preferred way of conducting his career:

> *"I'm definitely not the type of person . . . I don't have to live off of [beefs] like other artists. I didn't have to make*

a career off of that. My career is based off a solid foundation. It's not based off of calling out names like a 50 or whatever."

By "50," Nas is referring to artist 50 Cent, a notorious beefer who is always dissing other artists and forever in the middle of a heated situation with someone. Recently, he targeted Nas with his anger, and the two have been exchanging disses now for a while. Nas went on in the interview to say he actually feels bad about the situation with 50 Cent and sometimes wishes for the good old days when they were friends:

"You know what's the crazy thing about it? I've had times of missing 50. I brought him with me on tour before. He used to open up for me. I showed him his first Bentley. I showed him his first big diamonds in person. . . . So I kind of miss the cat from time to time. I would like to know what it is to sit down and talk to him, see what's on his mind. Because all he's showing is that when you get rich, you get angry at the world. And that's not what it's supposed to be about. I would love to really sit down with him. But on the rap side, we got things to finish. We got business—we got unfinished business."

The Most Controversial Move So Far

In 2006, however, hip-hop artists suddenly had a lot more to beef about, and they all seemed to be taking aim at Nas. That's because he released his eighth album, the controversial *Hip Hop Is Dead*. The title of the album sent other rappers into fits of rage. Suddenly it seemed like every rapper felt the title was a personal dig at them and their music. Nas didn't seem to mind the controversy, however, since it got everybody debating hip-hop and its current state and value—something he feels is in need of some serious analysis.

Hip Hop Is Dead dropped on December 19, 2006. It debuted at #1 on the *Billboard* 200 album chart and sold one million copies in less than a year. It also received a lot of glowing reviews, and for every rapper who has dissed Nas over the

As of January 2005, Nas is a married man. After a long relationship, he and Kelis, an R&B singer, were married. He also has a daughter. Family is important to Nas, and he wants to be a good role model for other black fathers.

album, another rapper has come faithfully to his side, declaring that the sentiments expressed in *Hip Hop Is Dead* are exactly what artists need to hear.

In the album's first single, "Hip Hop Is Dead," Nas mourns that in hip-hop, "Everybody sound the same, commercialize the game/Reminiscin' when it wasn't all business." One of the most surprising songs on the album, however, is a **collaboration** with Nas's old enemy, Jay-Z. The single is called "Black Republican," and it shows that rappers can accomplish more by uniting than by dissing.

On Fire for the Future

After more than fifteen years in the hip-hop game, Nas is hotter than ever. His career is on fire, and he's clearly found his place as an artist. But his chart-topping albums aren't the only things he has to be proud of. Today, Nas's family is the accomplishment in which he takes the most pride. On January 8, 2005, he married **R&B** singer Kelis, and in interviews he has stated that he couldn't be happier to be married. He also has a daughter, Destiny, from a previous relationship. In his songs and in interviews, Nas now talks about how important it is for black men to take their responsibilities to their families seriously, and he hopes that he will be a good role model in this respect.

As for future career plans, Nas says that hip-hop music isn't his only interest. Since early childhood, he has enjoyed reading, writing, and drawing. He never gave up those other interests. Now he'd like to pursue some of those things in the second half of his career. In an interview by the Associated Press, posted on sohh.com, he spoke about some of the things he'd still like to do:

"There's so much that I've never done. I love clothes, but I'm not excited about getting into the clothing business. I love sneakers, but not really excited about

doing it. My guys are interested in doing both clothes and sneakers that I might support . . . but what I'm really interested in is doing books and I like screenplays and I've written some, so you'll probably see some movies and stuff like that coming from me. Not from the big Hollywood end but on the independent end. I'm a student of filmmaking and not a student of the glitz of Hollywood. So you'll probably see something from me on the independent end and something really different on the novel end of the book level."

Nas is now writing some books and films, continuing to draw, and looking for other ways to let his "warrior spirit" out. In the sohh.com interview, he described himself as having a "warrior spirit" that motivates him to try to make a difference in the world. He also said that he believes black America needs more warrior spirits if the history of disenfranchisement that continues today is ever going to change. He used the "Vote or Die" campaign, spearheaded by P. Diddy and a number of other artists in 2004, as an example of good ideas that don't go far enough:

"I support Puff and anything he's doing dedicated to politics. I support his move, it was very Frank Sinatra, who was one of my heroes like when he supported the Kennedys . . . [but] I can't tell people to stand on line to vote and they're still going to be found in jail tomorrow. . . . [Black people] only do 12 percent of the crime in America but 70 percent of us get locked up. . . . I think Vote or Die is one way [to change things], but we have to pull other resources. . . . There is genius out there, when they go "Vote or Die" that's genius, but what's missing is that warrior spirit. There is a whole different spirituality that goes with the warrior spirit that Patrice Lumumba, Malcolm X, that they

In 2006, Nas released one of his most controversial albums, *Hip Hop Is Dead*. In this photo, Nas is shown celebrating its release at his Black and White Ball.

died for. Muhammad Ali had that. Richard Pryor had the warrior spirit. That's what's missing from hip-hop, and the only one that had it was Pac. I'm nowhere near the mind state he was. The stuff that he wrote, he was 21 years old and here I am 31 years old, and I'm still nowhere as deep as Tupac."

Clearly Nas is a man who has grown as an artist, and recognizes his potential as a leader, but still believes he has a long way to go. It's an admirable stance in a music world dominated by gangsta rhymes and bling. Nas has certainly explored those things in his long career. But in the end, he has risen up as a voice for education and self-empowerment. Perhaps his Web site, godsson.net, describes his work the best. It states that Nas's music is a "revolutionary message of faith, the streets, family, **retribution**, intelligence and rap's ultimate power." It's a message that connects hip-hop to its historical roots and gives it hope for a powerful future. It's a message that perhaps comes just in time.

1910–
1930 The Great Migration takes place.

1970s Hip-hop develops in the New York City borough of the Bronx.

Sept. 14,
1973 Nasir Jones, Nas, is born.

1980s The first popular rap songs hit the airwaves.

1988 N.W.A. is labeled the "World's Most Dangerous Group."

1991 Nas gets his first big break in music with an appearance on a Main Source song.

1994 Nas releases his first solo album.

1996 Nas releases his second solo album; it reaches the top of the charts.

1997 The Firm, a group consisting of Nas and other artists, releases its debut album; the crew breaks up soon after.

1998 Nas makes his film debut in *Belly*.

1999 *I Am . . .* debuts at #1 on the *Billboard* 200.

2000 Nas's label, Ill Will Records, releases an album featuring artists from Queensbridge Houses.

2004 *Street's Disciple* is released, which Nas considers some of his best work.

2005   Nas and R&B singer Kelis marry.

2006   Nas signs with Def Jam.

2006   Nas releases the controversial *Hip Hop Is Dead*.

Albums

1994 *Illmatic*

1996 *It Was Written*

1999 *I Am . . .*

1999 *Nastradamus*

2001 *Stillmatic*

2002 *God's Son*

2002 *The Best of Nas*

2004 *Street's Disciple*

2006 *Hip Hop Is Dead*

Number-One Single

1996 "Street Dreams" (Remix)

DVDs

2003 *Made You Look: God's Son Live*

2004 *Nas—Video Anthology, Vol. 1*

Film

1998   *Belly*

Book

Jones, Nasir. *Slave to a Page: The Book of Rhymes*. New York: Regan Books, 2007.

Awards and Recognition

1999   BET Awards: Best Rap Album (nominated).

Books

Bogdanov, Vladimir, Chris Woodstra, Steven Thomas Erlewine, and John Bush (eds.). *All Music Guide to Hip-Hop: The Definitive Guide to Rap and Hip-Hop.* San Francisco, Calif.: Backbeat Books, 2003.

Chang, Jeff. *Can't Stop Won't Stop: A History of the Hip-Hop Generation.* New York: Picador, 2005.

Emcee Escher and Alex Rappaport. *The Rapper's Handbook: A Guide to Freestyling, Writing Rhymes, and Battling.* New York: Flocabulary Press, 2006.

George, Nelson. *Hip Hop America.* New York: Penguin, 2005.

Jones, Nasir. *Slave to a Page: The Book of Rhymes.* New York: Regan Books, 2007.

Kusek, Dave, and Gerd Leonhard. *The Future of Music: Manifesto for the Digital Music Revolution.* Boston, Mass.: Berkley Press, 2005.

Light, Alan (ed.). *The Vibe History of Hip Hop.* New York: Three Rivers Press, 1999.

Waters, Rosa. *Hip-Hop: A Short History.* Broomall, Pa.: Mason Crest, 2007.

Watkins, S. Craig. *Hip Hop Matters: Politics, Pop Culture, and the Struggle for the Soul of a Movement.* Boston, Mass.: Beacon Press, 2006.

Web Sites

Nas
www.hiponline.com/artist/music/n/nas

Nas
www.godsson.net

Nas on Def Jam
www.defjam.com/site/artist_home.php?artist_id=608

Nas on VH1
www.vh1.com/artists/az/nas/bio.jhtml

Nas the Rapper
www.hip-hop-music-classic.com/Nas-the-Rapper.html

Glossary

collaboration—The act of working with someone to produce something.

commercial—Done with making a profit as the primary purpose.

compilation—Something created by gathering things from different sources.

credibility—Believability.

culture—The beliefs, customs, practices, and social behavior of a particular nation or people.

discriminatory—Treating a person or group unfairly, especially because of race, age, or gender.

diverse—Different from each other.

funk—A musical style that is based on jazz, blues, and soul and that is characterized by a heavy rhythmic bass and backbeat.

icon—Someone widely and uncritically admired as a symbol of a movement or field of activity.

intimidation—The act of persuading someone to do something or not to do something by fear.

mainstream—The ideas, actions, and values that are most widely accepted by a group or society.

mixtapes—Collections of songs recorded from other sources.

oppression—The condition of being dominated harshly by another person.

persona—The image of character and personality that someone wants to show the outside world.

platinum—A designation indicating that a recording has sold one million units.

R&B—Rhythm and blues; a style of music that combines elements of blues and jazz, and that was originally developed by African American musicians.

retribution—Something done or given to someone as punishment or revenge.

stereotypes—An oversimplified image, often based on incomplete and inaccurate information, held by one person or group about another.

tracks—Separate pieces of music on a disk, tape, or record.

underground—Separate from the main social or artistic environment.

Index

beef 39, 40, 47, 48
Belly 38
Breaking Atoms 34
"Black Republican" 50
"Bridging the Gap" 45

civil rights movement 26
Civil War 16, 20, 22

Def Jam 47

"Ether" 41

50 Cent 48

God's Son 41–42
Grandmaster Flash and the Furious Five 17
The Great Migration 21–22

Harlem 21–22
Harlem Renaissance 22
"Hate Me Now" 39
hip-hop 12–17
    as "Angry Music" 17
    as "Black Music" 15–16
    history of 12–17
Hip Hop is Dead 50

I Am 39
"I Can" 41–42

Illmatic 37–38
It Was Written 38

Jay-Z 39, 40, 47

"Live at the Barbeque" 34
The Lost Tapes 39
lynching 22, 25

Main Source 34
Malcolm X, 26
Martin Luther King, Jr. 26
"The Message" 17

Nas
    and beef with Jay-Z 39–41
    childhood 30–33
    and contradiction 10–11
    and Def Jam 47
    and 50 Cent 48
    and his father 31–33, 45
    and his mother 41
    and his "warrior spirit" 51
    and Ill Will 33–35
    and Ill Will Records 39
    as Kid Wave 32–33
    and Kelis 50
    and Mafioso Rap 38
    and Queensbridge 29, 31, 33, 35

Nas and Ill Will Records Present QB's Finest 39
Nastradamus 39
New York City 12, 14, 21, 24, 29, 30, 34, 52
N.W.A 17

"Poppa Was a Player" 33
Puff Daddy/P. Diddy 39, 50

Queens 29, 30
Queensbridge Houses 29, 30, 31, 33, 35, 39

racism 17, 20, 22, 23, 25, 26, 27

slavery 20, 22
southern rap
Stillmatic 41
Street's Disciple 42–45

Vietnam War 14
Vote or Die Campaign 51
voting rights 16, 17

Watergate 14
"The Watermelon Song" 35–36
White Flight 23

About the Author

Author Janice Rockworth grew up in the eighties when hip-hop music was just gaining momentum on the popular music scene. She remembers as a child being shocked by the lyrics of early hip-hop group 2 Live Crew, and amused by the light-hearted music of DJ Jazzy Jeff and the Fresh Prince. After studying sociology at an all-women's college, she became interested in hip-hop's social, historical, and political significance. Today she is a fan of political, conscious, and other alternative hip-hop styles.

Picture Credits

Corbis: front cover, pp. 12, 18
istockphoto.com
    Griffin, Jeff: p. 44
    Hart, Eileen: p. 17
    Lowe, Shaun: p. 34
    Podgorsek, Simon: p. 13
    Viisimaa, Peeter: p. 24
    Zalcam, Daniella: p. 30
PR Photos: pp. 2, 8, 36
    Hatcher, Chris: p. 40
    Schwegler, Chris: pp. 28, 43
    Solarpix: p. 49
    Thompson, Terry: p. 46
    Wild 1: p. 52

To the best knowledge of the publisher, all other images are in the public domain. If any image has been inadvertently uncredited, please notify Harding House Publishing Service, Vestal, New York 13850, so that rectification can be made for future printings.